The Age of the Lily,
The High Time—After the Time

The Eternal Word,
the One God, the Free Spirit,
speaks through Gabriele,
as through all the prophets of God—
Abraham, Job, Moses, Elijah, Isaiah,

Jesus of Nazareth,

the Christ of God

The Age of the Lily, The High Time—After the Time

Gabriele,
The teaching prophetess and emissary of God in our time

*"The Age of the Lily,
The High Time—After the Time"
Gabriele, the teaching prophetess and emissary of God,
in July 2019*

1st Edition, December 2023

Max-Braun-Str. 2, 97828 Marktheidenfeld
www.gabriele-verlag.com
www.gabriele-publishing-house.com

Translated from the original German title:

„Das Lilienzeitalter, Die hohe Zeit – nach der Zeit"

The German edition is the work of reference
for all questions regarding the meaning of the contents.

Order No. S191TBEN

Printed by: KlarDruck GmbH, Marktheidenfeld, Germany

ISBN 978-3-96446-328-9

The Age of the Lily, The High Time—After the Time

According to the Will of the Eternal All-One God and of the divine Wisdom, Sophia, I, Gabriele, may pass on some words from the eternal law of life. In June of 2019, the Eternal revealed the following at the end of His mighty revelation:

Depending on the corresponding country, the chapter of the long darkness on this Earth will gradually brighten, and it will get sunnier, because the Earth will also be more light-filled.

An Earth that becomes more light-filled signifies the spiritual dawn and the beginning of the New Era.

A virgin Earth will emerge under the sign of My Son, the Co-Regent of the Kingdom of God, who as Jesus of Nazareth announced His coming: "I Come Soon."...

People of the New Era find the true God in their peace-loving nature and, on the new Earth, build the Kingdom of Peace under the Sign of the Lily—Sophia—of purity and freedom, of the love for God and neighbor. …

The gateway of the Lily, of the Wisdom, under the Sign of Sophia is opening. …

Already now, the call of the Christ of God goes around the Earth, and all people who bear the cross on their brow, the sign of peace and of love, hear the call of the Christ of God, which says: "Where two or three are gathered in My name, there am I, in the midst of them."

Further, the call of the Christ of God:

***"The signs are visible, the appearance
leads the way, the dawn
reveals to My own the light-filled day
and the New Era.
In God, My Father,
the eternal Being, I Am His Son.
The regency pair of eternal Wisdom makes
My coming manifest.***

***In this awareness of the New Era for
peace-loving people:
The Christ of God, who I Am in the eternal
Father-Mother-Being,
in God, who is the eternity!"***

Dear fellow people, we still live in a dark time, in which one is against the other, and the one who is still one with his neighbor is more or less a rarity.

What we people hear and read from the law, God, is a gift to us. The one who accepts it and practices it step-by-step feels where this positive All-Energy comes from.

Indeed, the Spirit of Truth, the Free Spirit, truly pours from the cornucopia of life, and the people who fulfill step by step the wisdoms from the Kingdom of God begin to come to life like a flower that is touched by a ray of sun.

The cornucopia, the energy of life, still holds much in store for us people, for example, the Lily of purity, of beauty and of the Wisdom of God—for a more light-filled time.

Who will join us? Who will go with us?

Very gradually and unnoticeably, we are entering the time in which the Lily begins to grow and blossom. It is the beginning of the unity of life in God, the Eternal.

Despite the over-exploitation of nature, it wants to radiate the life to us people. The stars and planets as well, especially on a starlit night, have a lot to say to us.

Nature can also be seen as a garden in us. The countless symphonies of the flowers, the bushes, the trees, the grasses are a symphony, like a melody in us. The life in God wants to touch us and communicate with us because everything is communication.

Communication with the true life in us means to gradually learn and experience that we human beings are the temple of God that shines in us in countless facets. The temple of which Jesus of Nazareth spoke is an inestimable garden in us. It is the essence of the Kingdom of God, which is our homeland.

And when we try to connect with the planets on a starlit night, we experience that we are not from this dark world.

In the end, we are merely wayfarers to the Kingdom of God, to our eternal homeland, and thus, merely guests on this Earth.

To where are we going?

What is our goal?

Each day, every hour and every minute shows us where we are going and how we are preparing our pathways.

Although the still dark time attempts to reel us in again and again—as revealed—we are going step by step into the Age of the Lily, into the high time.

One morning—after the dark time—the time will have come for the deep dawn to open and indicate the new day, the New Era, the high time. It is the Spirit of the Christ of God, the life that He announced as Jesus of Nazareth.

What is the goal of a person striving toward God?

As already stated: God in us. With time, the prayers of "God in us," reach the proximity of our physical heart, where the ray of the Christ of God shines.

After every deep heart-prayer "God in us," we learn and experience what it means to experience God in us and to learn, because we gradually become aware of what the All-communication means, for God, the life, is in everything that lives. Communication is a conscious, omnipresent life.

With time, we experience more and more that we are not alone. A kind, loving Spirit, the Spirit of our heavenly Father, goes with us. He is in us—God.

Regardless of where our gaze falls, which causes us to linger somewhat longer—we experience that everything lives, everything has content. There is nothing that is dead. With time—since practice makes perfect—we feel and experience that everything is based on communication. Consequently, every person is a sender and receiver.

Once we become aware of this, that everything sends and that we can receive according to our radiation, then we also understand the word "caution," because everything else also sends and wants to establish contact with us to the extent that we are reachable.

As long as we live in the still dark time, there is need for "caution." Where should we let caution prevail, that is, to what should we pay attention? To our feelings and thoughts, to our wanting and desires!

The dark time has egomania in itself. None of us is totally free of it, for example, of envy, enmity, wanting to have, all the way to greed, etc., etc.

The dark time also bears other enticements, for example, being self-opinionated in order to thus determine others. The craving for recognition is also a driving force that has many and varied expressions.

What is it like if a person categorically wants to climb higher on the ladder to success? In doing so, trampling others underfoot is not a rarity.

Many more such expressions "to below" could be enumerated.

On hearing the words "to below," the word "subconscious" automatically comes up.

The subconscious is a collector. Everything that we do not want to or cannot express, regardless of reason, goes into the subconscious. The subconscious can be compared to a mixing board. Our programs that are stored there for the time being, that which we had in our thoughts and did not want to or could not express, is placed by the collector on the subconscious, which can also be seen as a mixing board. What we want to express, the subconscious then brings into the conscious mind. Now we express it or act accordingly. What comes of this is not by chance—it comes from us. Much of what I do not want to mention here, but only briefly suggest, is what we have input ourselves.

We are the one—and none other.

What we attribute to or think toward others or even carried out as actions of the worst kind is what we ourselves are.

Where is the point of access that we are not aware of? It is our subconscious that collects and mixes, the contents of which we can call up. There are many opportunities, because the day has many different facets.

Especially self-control and self-observation can be helpful in order to find ourselves.

Indifference and complacency, in particular, lead to the torpor of our disposition and mind. All this and more are the points of entry.

The one who believes in the eternal truth and keeps the Ten Commandments of God through Moses and the Sermon on the Mount of Jesus of Nazareth has done the right thing and knows to where his path leads.

We people simply are not perfect, but when and how our path will merge into perfection is something we determine ourselves.

Despite all this, in the very basis of the soul, we are sons and daughters of perfection. Jesus of Nazareth taught us: *Be perfect, as your eternal Father in heaven is perfect.*

If we want to return to perfection, to the eternal homeland, then, as stated, it is necessary to set goals.

To the people in all the generations, Jesus of Nazareth, the Christ of God, brought the teachings that were meant to be applied. If humankind had accepted the teachings of Jesus, the Christ, ultimately to let the Kingdom of God resurrect in the soul and in the person, then every ensouled human being would be consciously filled with the spirit, and his existence on Earth would be meaningful.

Then there would no longer be the dice of horror that goes by the name of death and trigger fears as to when the hour might come. Instead, there would be the attitude that considers density, matter, as merely a transformation, which implies: The physical body departs from this world, and the soul sets off on the further path toward perfection, just as Jesus of Nazareth taught us: *Be perfect, as your eternal Father in heaven is perfect.*

Our further path then leads to the Father who is in heaven—that is, directly into the Kingdom of God, to our eternal homeland, and not over the times in the times, which possibly implies reincarnations, that is, human births.

If we take the trouble to consider this, then we would have to ask ourselves: Whom have we followed in all the years, let alone the last two thousand years?

There are enough excuses for why it is the way it is.

But let us ask ourselves if we had no orientation at all?

And if we did, then why did we not accept this path, for example, the Ten Commandments of God through Moses and the teachings of Jesus of Nazareth, His Sermon on the Mount and His indication: *The Kingdom of God is within, in you*?

Or: Why did we let the teachings of the messengers of God who brought the eternal word of the Being be rejected and became followers of a religion and a god of religion?

Or: Why did we contribute to religious deputies carrying out the command of religions, for example, as with Jesus of Nazareth, the state power, which until today carries out the command of the teachers of religion?

With certainty, many a one will say, "I live today, and today is simply today." Who can prove that we did not live as human beings yesterday as well, and the day before yesterday, that is, during the past 2000 years after Jesus of Nazareth?

We can say, and rightly so: That cannot be proven!

That's right! No one can prove that he has already often taken on a human body during the times of times before Jesus of Nazareth, but also after Jesus of Nazareth.

This and other questions string together like pearls on a chain:

Why are we followers of religions, of which Jesus of Nazareth never taught?

Why do we adhere to a guild of priests, which interfered already with Moses—as we can see by the fact that with Moses, there is the "Priestly Source"—when Jesus of Nazareth never installed any priests?

Why do we believe in churches of stone heavy with riches, with embellishments of gold and silver and all sorts of trumpery, when Jesus of Nazareth spoke in a different way?

Why do we believe in anathemas all the way to an alleged eternal damnation, when Jesus of Nazareth did not teach such things—nor the Eternal All-One God through His divine messengers?

Why does a person let himself be bound to religions or their beliefs, when all he has to do is merely to believe in this religious expert teaching—which, however, cannot be proven at all from religion to religion?

We people need to ask ourselves these and other questions if we want to attain clarity about ourselves.

The statements of Fyodor Dostoevsky can help us with this. In his novel about the brothers Karamazov, in the chapter "The Grand Inquisitor," he speaks to the one who appeared again in Seville, Jesus of Nazareth:

"Why, then, have You come to hinder us? For You have come to hinder us, and You know that. But do You know what will be tomorrow? I know not who You are and care not to know whether it is You or only a semblance of Him, but tomorrow I shall condemn You and burn You at the stake as the worst of heretics. And the very people who have today kissed Your feet, tomorrow at the faintest sign from me will rush to heap up the embers of Your fire. Know You that? Yes, maybe You know it," he added with thoughtful penetration, never for a moment taking his eyes off the Prisoner …

"Do You have the right to reveal to us one of the mysteries of that world from which You have come?" the Grand Inquisitor asks Him, and answers the question for himself. "No, You have not;

that You may not add to what has been said of old, and may not take from men the freedom which You did exalt when You were on earth.

Whatsoever You reveal anew will encroach on men's freedom of faith; for it will be manifest as a miracle, and the freedom of their faith was dearer to You than anything in those days fifteen hundred years ago. Did You not often say then, 'I will make you free'? But now You have seen these free men! ...

Yes, we have paid dearly for it," the Great Inquisitor goes on, looking sternly at the reappeared Jesus, "but at last we have completed that work in Your name. For fifteen centuries we have been wrestling with Your freedom, but now it is ended and over for good. Do You not believe that it is over for good? You look meekly at me and deign not even to be wrathful with me. But let me tell You that now, today, people are more persuaded than ever that they have perfect freedom, yet they have brought their freedom to us and laid it humbly at our feet. But that has been our doing. Was this Your freedom that You desired? ...

But only one who can appease their conscience can take over their freedom. In bread there was offered You an invincible banner; give bread, and man will worship You, for nothing is more certain than bread. But if someone else gains possession of his conscience—Oh! then he will cast away Your bread and follow after him who has appeased his conscience. …

Instead of taking possession of men's freedom, You did increase it, and burdened the spiritual kingdom of mankind with its sufferings forever. You did desire man's free love, that he should follow You freely, enticed and taken captive by You. In place of the rigid ancient law, man must hereafter with free heart decide for himself what is good and what is evil, having only Your example before him as his guide. …

There are three powers, three powers alone, able to conquer and to hold captive forever the conscience of these impotent rebels for their happiness. And those forces are miracle, mystery and authority. …

We have corrected Your work and have founded it upon miracle, mystery and authority. And men rejoiced that they were again led like sheep, and that the terrible gift that had brought them such suffering, was, at last, lifted from their hearts. Were we right teaching them this? Speak! Did we not love mankind, so meekly acknowledging their feebleness, lightening their burden and permitting their weak nature even to sin with our sanction?

Why have You come now to hinder us? And why do You look silently and searchingly at me with Your mild eyes? Be angry. I don't want Your love, for I love You not. And what use is it for me to hide anything from You? Don't I know to Whom I am speaking? All that I can say is known to You already, I can read it in Your eyes.

And is it for me to conceal from You our mystery? Perhaps it is Your will to hear it from my lips. Listen then: We are not working with You, but with him—that is our mystery. It is long—eight centuries …

Just eight centuries ago, we took from him ... what You did reject with scorn, that last gift he offered You, showing You all the kingdoms of the earth. We took from him Rome and the sword of Caesar, and proclaimed ourselves rulers of the earth, though we have not yet been able to complete our work. ...

I repeat, tomorrow You shall see that obedient flock who at a sign from me will hasten to heap up the hot cinders about the pile on which I shall burn You for coming to hinder us. For if anyone has ever deserved our fires, it is You. Tomorrow I shall burn You."

(From "The Grand Inquisitor," a chapter of the novel "The Brothers Karamazov" by Fyodor Dostoevsky)

If we are to understand everything according to its meaning, as we are advised in the revelations of God, then it is clear that it is the contents of the words that make sense. The same is also true then, for every written word and also for the spoken word.

How often do we and our fellow people say and hear: "Did I understand that right?" Or: "Did you mean it this way?"

Each one of us has to ask himself the question, in terms of what he placed into his words and what he meant by it.

Each one can put into the same word his own meaning, thus, what he wants to express with it. This is why the question is often asked: "Will I be understood like this?"

Each one of us places into the word, be it read or heard, whatever corresponds to our momentary consciousness. Every statement too, we grasp according to the state of our consciousness. And we ourselves place into our words, that is, statements, what corresponds to our momentary consciousness. Thus, each one speaks himself, according to his present state of consciousness.

Therefore, the request from me, Gabriele: Please understand my words according to their meaning.

Basically, it can be said that nothing, but really nothing, can be proven by us human beings. And we frequently speak past each other. Each one speaks himself, and each one reads out of a book or a writing only that which corresponds to his momentary state of consciousness.

What does state of consciousness mean?

I compare the brain as such with a matrix. What is stored in our brain is our present state; it is our momentary consciousness, the same as a matrix.

What is said to us or what we read, we take into the cells of our brain for the time being.

As stated: I compare our brain with a matrix. What we hear or read is placed onto the matrix within seconds, onto what we have already input and stored, and it mixes with what is already in the brain—then we understand only what the brain signals to us.

The same is true when we respond to something.

In the end, we understand and answer only what our memory bank, the brain, gives—in this case, without the mixing board, the subconscious.

This is simply how it is. Self-evidence provides the corresponding answer.

Everything that we say, read or hear cannot be proven. We human beings believe what we take in through the lens of our consciousness. This, too, cannot be proven, because each one can understand from what was said or read only what they have stored in their brain.

Therefore, "The Age of the Lily, The High Time—After the Time."

If it is about belief, we are the ones called upon: Do we go step by step into the high and light-filled time and build on the All-Unity, on the law of God, on the omnipresent life—or do we believe what others believe and opine?

The help from the Spirit of God: The law of the love for God and neighbor gives the following indication, so as to understand the words according to their meaning.

"To understand according to their meaning" means to draw closer to the truth, the eternal law, God, in all things. This means: not having to believe, but knowing.

It is not for nothing that Jesus of Nazareth said: *The Kingdom of God is within, in you.*

Or: *Seek first the Kingdom of God and all else will be given to you.*

Or: *Be perfect as your eternal Father in heaven is perfect.*

No one can take from us our faults and the imperfection that came about through them.

We, each one of us, is asked, what we want to do about it.

No religion can take from us what we have burdened ourselves with—regardless of the name with which the guild of priests presents itself.

Everything that the individual person speaks or writes is understood and interpreted by another according to his consciousness.

Because it is the way it is, I will endeavor with my further explanations concerning the question of "why," to leave the answer open to each reader or listener himself.

Why does the person who belongs to a certain church faith have to pay for religious services if everything cannot even be proven?

Whoever now thinks about it will continue with the question: Did Jesus of Nazareth found a church of stone, suggest priests or pastors or the like or even install them?

If not, then who was it?

Nor did Jesus of Nazareth command the dictator of faith Luther to encourage so-called Lutherans to "sin boldly."

Who was it that established such rules?

And why should a person who is a member of a certain faith go to confession, depending on the ecclesiastical regulation?

If a believer is absolved of his confessed sins by a priest or pastor, then he should be free of them. Why does the one who was absolved from his confessed sins commit the same sins again after one day or days later?

After the allegedly remedied lapse into sin, the sinner then takes the so-called consecrated host—allegedly the body of Christ—that is, a communion wafer offered possibly by the same priest who yesterday or the day before had absolved him of his confessed sins.

Jesus of Nazareth taught according to the following: to clear things up with our neighbor as long as we are on the way with him. And that each one is the temple of God because God, the All-Life, dwells in us.

Whoever thinks about all that and takes his steps continues pondering:

Did Jesus of Nazareth recommend that we take a consecrated host or consecrated wine as the "body" or the "blood" of Christ?

If yes, then with this, Jesus, the Christ, would be rescinding His Last Supper with His disciples, and certainly also with His female disciples, in favor of a religion.

At the Last Supper Jesus essentially said to do as He had done with all of them.

From the great Christ-revelation "This Is My Word, Alpha and Omega," I quote some words of revelation on the Last Supper. The Spirit of the Christ of God Himself revealed the following to us people:

Translators can interpret the texts only with their vocabulary, which corresponds to their state of consciousness. Furthermore, the translations could not and cannot always be made according to the meaning of the word, since the same words can have a different meaning for each person—according to his consciousness and his conception. Thus, in many cases, My word, also My word as Jesus of Nazareth, was seen with the lens of faith of those who passed it on. ...

As Jesus of Nazareth, I often prayed to God, My Father, and dialogued with Him. I prayed to Him, the Eternal, for the blessing of the Last Supper with My own.

I spoke to them as follows: Continue to do in My memory what I now do. The food is for the body. I offer it to you as a symbol for inner strengthening.

Recognize that My body is sacrificed, so that you may attain eternal life. Let your body become a temple, so that the Spirit may be active in and through you. Through the resurrection of My spiritual body, you, too, will resurrect; for the Christ of God, who goes to the Father, is the Spirit of truth in God. The Spirit of truth will purify your spiritual body, and the light of the world, which I Am, will shine in and through you. For through My resurrection, I Am the light in you and the purification of your soul. The one who believes in Me and fulfills the laws of the heavens will attain rebirth in the Spirit of My Father through Me, the Christ.

I took the wine, added some water to it and spoke as follows: What I tell you now is a symbol. Recognize the meaning and think of Me while you eat and drink; for in all things is the Spirit of life, who I Am.

The wine is the symbol of My blood, which I will shed for all souls and men. The Spirit of the soul must be awakened again by soul and person, that is, it must be brought into the earthly life. The soul of the one who does not accept and receive the Spirit of truth—as a symbol, it is My blood—cannot return to eternity, because it does not live in the absolute truth. The soul remains outside heaven until it has accepted and received Me, the light of the world, its Redeemer. Thus, the one who does not accept and receive Me, his Redeemer, the Co-Regent of the heavens, will not attain absolute perfection.

Recognize that the one who does not accept and receive Me does not accept and receive the Father either, for the Father and I are one.

I, in Jesus of Nazareth, carried out this symbolic event among My own, in order to explain to them that the life, the Spirit of God, is in all forms of life as substance and power. …

Ask for God's blessing for your meal and, while eating, think of the power and love of God, and you will also think of your Redeemer, the Christ of God, who is in the Father.

(From the great work of revelation of the Christ of God: "This Is My Word, Alpha and Omega")

The Christ of God is the power in the Father-Mother-Being and in the All-Life, which we take as food and drink. This is why followers of Christ pray before their meal, in order to partake of the food and drink in His name. After eating, they give thanks for the food and drink. Christ-followers respect the life that nature gives. They do not partake of anything that has a breath, that is, they let it live.

They reject any animal massacre that brings down the animals on the fields and in the woods with the sacrificial cudgel, as well as any consumption of meat of the animals that are sacrificed by being fattened in barns for the lust of the palate. People in the spirit of life, which is the truth, do not go through their fields to spread poison, quite the contrary.

Before harvest, communication with the fields is called for. They often go to the fields and take up communication with the fruit and the animals in the fields, for everything is based on sending and receiving. Through the All-communication, which is the All-Being, the radiation of the fruit and in the animals of the field is raised, which to them, the animals, is a signal to leave the field before harvest.

This is why the followers of Christ leave behind a strip of the field with standing fruit. With this, the animals are given the possibility to find shelter for themselves in the field.

This, too, is part of the general prayer, for prayer should always be focused on the unity, because God, the Eternal, is the All-Unity.

The human being is, of course, also a part of the All-Unity. And in this sense, the question arises: Up to what milestone do the so-called Christian values extend?

Many people disregard the teachings of Jesus of Nazareth because most of them have bound themselves to religious customs. Religious customs are just simply "customs," of which Jesus of Nazareth did not speak. Nevertheless, religious customs are often improperly termed "Christian values" because, among other things, many a state power subordinates itself to a religion and its customs. Then the sacramental state power calls itself "Christian" and adorns itself with so-called "Christian values."

Whether one merely calls oneself Christian or honestly endeavors to strive in daily life for true Christian values would be an inexhaustible topic.

To work out the difference between church doctrine with its religious customs and true Christian values, the Ten Commandments of

God and the Sermon on the Mount of Jesus of Nazareth would be important, as would an unraveled and understandable Lord's Prayer.

If we want to reflect more on the so-called "Christian values," then we could once again turn to the Ten Commandments of God. Suddenly the fifth commandment is now supposed to read: *You shall not murder.* From the very beginning it was: *You shall not kill.* The distortion of meaning also has its significance here, when weapons are produced under the specific seal of "Christian values."

It would also be advisable to think about it again at the right time and at the right hour.

To remain faithful to the old times, to the sinful aspects and to the wordplays of a religion, pastors and priests act by pouring so-called baptismal water over the head of an infant.

Here, too, the question is: what did Jesus of Nazareth teach?

Jesus of Nazareth never deprived us of our free will, by absorbing freedom into a religion with a trickle of water. Jesus of Nazareth taught the Free Spirit and not coercion, let alone the constraint of baptism under the religious threat: “If not baptized, then …!”

When people decide about their infant or toddler and incorporate the child into a religion, then usually the first step is infant baptism, baptism by water.

Everyone is free and will act according to their state of consciousness.

In the great Christ-Revelation “This Is My Word, Alpha and Omega,” we can read the following concerning this:

However, the one who has developed the love for God and for his neighbor is raised by the Spirit of God, that is, he is imbued with the Spirit of truth. The one who is spiritually mature needs fewer and fewer symbols and ceremonies. He lives in the inner being, just as it is in heaven: pure! The pure one is filled with the Spirit of truth and imbued with the Spirit of life: He is thus baptized by the Spirit of God. …

With the words "teach and then baptize," I meant baptism by the Holy Spirit, because the one who has received and fulfilled the teachings of the Spirit is the spiritually baptized one; he no longer needs baptism by water. Baptism by water can now be seen merely as a symbol, because every person who actualizes the laws of God is baptized by the Spirit of life and can enter heaven because he fulfills the law of life, God in Me, the Christ, more and more. …

Several so-called Christian denominations force their faithful into baptism with water. Even the little children whose free will is not yet developed and who therefore cannot yet decide for themselves are forced, with baptism by water, into the membership of a church and thereby induced to participate in its other rituals. This is an infringement of the individual's free will and a forced Christianization, so to speak. …

It is written, "… and He remained there and baptized many." The word "baptism" means the blessing of the heart, of the inner being, through the Holy Spirit. I saw into the hearts of My own and recognized that those who lived in the actualization of the laws of God increased the light and the power of God in themselves every day. My blessing caused further seeds of inner life to grow in them and caused them to strive towards perfection in order to pass on to the people what they actualized in and on themselves, in their present earthly life and in further incarnations. …

Recognize that only the spiritual baptism is valid. Everything else is symbols, and, as such, have no meaning or validity, because they are not part of the law of God. I did not institute the ritual blessing, anointing and offering of the fruits of the Earth as external ceremonies. It is spoken as a symbol for the inner life and not meant as an outer ceremony.

(From the great work of revelation of the Christ of God: "This Is My Word, Alpha and Omega")

Ultimately, each one of us must choose for himself what he wants to do and whom he believes. Nothing is provable, not even belief. Each one himself can check—but also check himself, in terms of whom he believes.

My personal answer to this: We can merely believe—no one can prove it.

This also applies to me: What I write or say, what God, the Eternal, and the law-beings reveal through me, His prophetess, I cannot prove.

What God revealed before Abraham and after Abraham up to the present time, through prophets and prophetesses and through many, countless communities in all generations—no one can prove. Nor can a religious guild—no matter what mission it purports to have—prove what it proclaims to its paying people.

The state power, which in many cases is the lackey of a religious guild, cannot prove what it mandates in the name of a religion.

Can a state at all prove that what it enacts is right?

Perhaps one opines quite succinctly: It can do that! But if the state can actually do that, then the question automatically comes up: Has the sacred state-horse imposed climate change on the people, under which unspeakable suffering is already taking place, especially to the animal and plant worlds? Or is the animal merely a thing, as many a state differential thinks?

Here is a remark by someone who has heard and watched our radio and television programs for a long time:

Law proposals from animal protectors for an improved system of animal protection fail again and again also because of the political parties that call themselves "Christian," which declare the animal protection paragraphs anchored in the law to be sufficient.

What mockery, what cynicism, what testimony of spiritual poverty is illustrated in this attitude, when you think of the millions upon millions of animals that are skinned and dismembered alive! Not to even mention the often bestial animal husbandry.

Yet to the suffering of animals, delegates of an apparently ethically and morally low-minded people sit in the parliaments and often contribute to the debates with their Catholic or Lutheran pattern, that is, nothing but hollow animal protection clichés. However, these Catholic and Lutheran patterns ultimately mean: war against God's creatures, war against the animals!

Anyone who believes that the ideology of the Catechism has less influence outside the churches should take note of the following quotation from an avowedly and particularly Catholic Christian Social Union (CSU) member of the German Parliament from May 17, 2002:

"It's no secret that for a long time we have fought against anchoring animal protection in our Constitution ... because there have always been efforts to give our constitution in its basic orientation an eco-centric orientation.

In our opinion ... the human being is the sole legal person of our legal system. There has always been an attempt to also grant rights to plants, animals and other elements of creation and to nature as a whole. ... According to our understanding, animals are our fellow creatures ... but not legal persons. In this sense, they are not an individual. ...

The animal has no obligations toward human beings. Therefore, it also has no claim toward human beings for a species-appropriate care. The possible difficulties in economy and research were not the reason for our reluctance. Rather, our concern was and is that the human being remain the focus of the Constitution."

By the way, the Catholic member of the German Parliament also had bestowed upon him the Pontifical Order of St. Gregory the Great, granted for his zeal in defense of the Catholic religion!

(End of the remarks from a radio listener and television viewer)

Dear fellow people, if it were so that the animal is merely a thing, then the question arises: Do human beings not give the animals a voice, or rights, as stated, because the animal might be taking the air, the breath, away from the human beings? Or is it because the animals are not Catholic?

Should the animals have to prove a religious affiliation, or should one of the animals perhaps have to have a pontifical medal, in order to have a right to life, to a species-appropriate care?

Or is the breath of a human being more valuable because he believes—whereby here we are again with belief—that due to the "expensive" windmills he is entitled to more energy, perhaps even more air, that is, breath, than the "object animal"?

Perhaps a just barely tolerable percentage-wise suffocation quota for the city dwellers should be legally determined—for example, how many deaths by suffocation per thousand inhabitants—because, after all, everything should serve the state and the religions.

A scientific calculation of how much oxygen the animals simply breathe away from humans without permission and how this compares in proportion to factory farming, to meat consumption, that is, to animal cannibalism, to the acidification of the oceans, to the dying forests and the resulting ever-decreasing oxygen content in the air, is getting to be more and more urgent and probably will not be long in coming due to the rapidly progressing climate change.

Everything is based on the revenues of the state and the ancillary belief in state and church.

Everyone is free to choose.

Dear fellow people, choose for yourselves! In all of infinity there is no coercion, except in the coercive pressure of religion, which tries, in a procedure of power, to implant its god into the conscience of its believers—which it does, among other things, on the premise that the horse serves the rider as a beadle.

Who pays for this—the state, the church, or the people?

Now you could think: What is Gabriele trying to tell us?

Dear fellow people, nothing, because nothing can be proven.

What I carry in my heart, not in my hands, is the proof that God, the Eternal, exists, that God, the Eternal, is the All-Love and a caring heavenly Father who wants all His sons and daughters back home again.

Because I know this, the call of Jesus of Nazareth affects me deeply:

Come all to Me, I want to lead you to the eternal Father who is in heaven.

Nothing can be proven, including His call.

Therefore, my suggestion: Prove it to yourself.

Try to find the center of your life and you will understand what the call of Jesus, the Christ, means. What you experience and learn is your proof. You cannot prove this to another person. Live the life, God, without much fuss.

There is a time for everything.

Eventually, people will come together who have found Him, the Eternal, the All-Love, and let the day become the day that radiates to them the dawn of the new day. It is the life that shows the new person what true responsibility means—without religion, solely through true eternal love, which no longer knows the "ego shadow" and which is: God in us, the life.

Then the dawn will define the daylight, and a mild sun will shine on the people who fulfill the "Let there be," in which it says: Let it become—a new heaven and a new Earth under the sign of the Lily—God in us.

Then the new human being has risen who understands the words of freedom of the spiritual Messiah: Come all and let it become, as in heaven very gradually so on Earth.

Dear fellow people, be daring!

Choose freely and without being compelled to believe, God, the life, God, the love, in each one of us.

May I just give you a few tips about how I found the life in God, our Father, and that, as a human being all alone, albeit with the divine teacher, the spirit being, who prepared me for the word of life, in order to pass it on:

In the spirit of love, of eternal life, which is given for the New Era, it is the Age of the Lily, of freedom, also called the Messianic, Sophianic Age.

My life should be nothing other than an indication *for* the life.

My path is the life in God that says: I love God, our eternal heavenly Father, and put Him first in my feeling and thinking, in all my behavior. Why? Because I love Him.

What I pass on here, I cannot prove—nor do I want to prove it. Try it out yourself. You decide, yes or no. It is up to you.

I have already reported on the following event. The repetition, when given in other words, can, with other indications, now give an "aha-experience" to many a person, because it was similar for them.

Before I had found God in me, there was a, for me, terrible event; it could also be seen as a sign or as guidance.

The years passed in which I searched for God. No one could convince me that God exists. I did not want others to tell me that God exists; I wanted to prove it to myself.

After years of searching in both prayer and nature, I found God in myself. I cannot prove that, but I can give a word of advice: Try it out yourself. You are your own personal proof yourself.

Happy the person who forgets what is many a sacrifice in everyday life.

In retrospect, I can say that I sacrificed nothing, merely my bad aspects, my bad thoughts, my veiled expressions, and my selfish will, which strove for recognition and to be loved, if not to say, demanded it. Only the sacrifice of egoism makes a person happy and brings him close to God.

If you want, try it—you are not alone; a good, kind Spirit goes with you: God, the Spirit of our heavenly Father.

God's love for His sons and daughters, for His children, is boundless.

A genuinely deep and heartfelt attempt to draw closer to God, to the life in us, is truly worthwhile!

Be patient with yourself. In time, you will become calmer and more prudent. The so-called narrative arts—communicating with others in order to perhaps gain enhancement and recognition—will decrease. You become more helpful because you become more straightforward with yourself and then, with your neighbor, more honest and more goal-oriented.

Soon, you will notice how you have lied to yourself until now, because you become more aware of your subcommunications. You become more sure of yourself.

Our subcommunications are sending potentials. They go out from ourselves and build up, for example, when we speak. This happens as if automatically. For example, when we speak and do not want to express certain thoughts. We hold back what we do not want to say.

Everything is based on energy.

What we don't want to say goes into our subconscious and runs alongside, especially when we are speaking. What has not been spoken, but which we thought, regardless of reason, remains in the subconscious. In this way, corresponding sending potentials are built up in the subconscious, which can also affect our nervous system and make us restless or even nervous and, not least, draw on our day's energy. In time, we live more and more oriented to our personal aspects.

With this, we grow energetically weaker and more indifferent. The indifference all too readily aligns with the concepts of others. In time, we do not realize that we can be influenced, even if by our own sending potential, the subconscious.

Therefore: change your thinking in time! However, this is not possible from one day to the next. As the saying goes: Practice makes perfect. Yet, this does not mean to gain mastery over others, but over ourselves!

Which now brings us to Patience, an attribute of God from the three attributes of filiation. In our words, they are called:

Patience, Love and Mercy.

In the All-Law, God, the three attributes of God are called Kindness, Love and Meekness. These are the filiation attributes of the Father-Mother-God, of the Father-Mother-Being. To reawaken them and build them up again means to change our thinking.

The spiritual anchor for people on their way to the New Era is called: the Lily, Sophia, the Wisdom of God.

The Lily is purity in feeling, thinking and speaking. The Wisdom in God is His work of the deed in all Being. This means to be active in the right way.

God, the All-Life, is the beauty in all things.

We are called upon to prove to ourselves that God exists.

Wisdom, God's work of the deed, is, among other things, also the sense of responsibility in us for everything that we think, speak and do. Thus, we are called upon: A conscientious yes to God is also the yes to ourselves, to fulfill the eternal law, God.

Anything else would be self-deception. I also think thereby of many a remark by my fellow people, who state as a matter of course: People kid themselves.

That's how it is: No one knows himself, and that's why he often doesn't know what he's really saying—contingent on his personal subconscious.

Or: Everyone talks past the other one.

Or: Everyone speaks himself.

In the end, everything that is spoken so succinctly lacks proof.

Nothing can be proven that comes from people.

When two people converse, the one does not know what the other puts into his words, and vice versa.

Each one of us has his specific inputs, which, on the one hand, shape him and on the other hand, determine him, depending on the sending potential in his conscious mind and in the subconscious.

I am a human being who places God, the Father-Mother-God, the Being in the Being, the All-Law, God, above all things, especially the three attributes Kindness, Love and Meekness.

Perhaps you experience something similar, therefore, the repetition:

After a long search I found God in me, and that, after a blow of fate and years of searching. Again and again, I asked my fellow people about God. No one could really tell me whether God existed. In conversation with acquaintances, I heard in passing: "God in us."

Aha, therefore, God in me! Who is God?

I thought and thought: "God in me" can only be the strength in me.

That was again the feeling I often had in nature, which prompted me to pray.

Before, my prayers were awkward, more like prayers of supplication than prayers of thanksgiving. Mostly, they revolved around me.

If you also want to try it, from my own experience, a word of advice and a suggestion:

Go into nature to watch how the wind gently and softly moves the grasses, or how inexpressibly many flowers, grasses and herbs live together and how the grass or blade of grass helps a flowering plant to stand upright as long as possible.

Or, for example, how the dandelion blossoms —one of the first manifestations of spring— change and the wind spreads countless seeds.

Who intervenes in the many processes, from spring to autumn? Nature knows about this. In many cases, humankind brutally intervenes in the life of nature and crushes the life that is revealing itself. It is different when animals go through the enchantment of nature—either the life in nature straightens up again or it sacrifices itself to the feet of the animals.

And what about the two-legged ones?

For example, in autumn the leaves fall from the deciduous trees. Does the tree complain, or does it surrender to the cycle of the year?

The tree knows that autumn is merely a transition, so as to continue to grow in the same form of existence in spring.

Whether sunshine or rain or snow, nature gratefully accepts everything—it knows of the mighty All-Creator-God in all things.

We notice similar things in the animal world. The animals know about the change of coats and feathers and about the time for reproduction.

What about human beings? Does the human being orient himself to the law of order and the rule of moderation?

Or: Anyone who watches the ripe fields in summer and how the human being deals with them should ask himself: How does the ripe crop feel when people come thundering over the fields with huge machines?

I watched many things. As time went by, I thought, "I am not a part of this cruelty in the woods and meadows, on the fields and in the fattening pens of livestock breeding."

More and more, I began to pray into myself: God in me! I gained access to myself—God in me—until several years later, a wise being touched me and led me to accept what I had said yes to—as it has been stated in many divine revelations: the training to be a prophet. But all in all: My roots are grounded in God in me!

To be a prophet is a divine mission, but nothing else.

I am in God because God is in me.

I affirm and keep what is God's Will, from the divine Order all the way to Mercy.

Because I live in the consciousness of God, the All-power in me, I especially love, as stated, the three filiation attributes: Kindness, Love and Meekness.

Nature shows this to me.

For me, the three filiation attributes are like a magnet that attracts me again and again, and that resonate in the words for the New Era—the Age of the Lily, Sophia, the Wisdom of God.

Dear fellow people, in the Age of the Lily, the motto is: Try it out and find God, the eternal Love, in yourself.

We human beings are used to holding fast, mainly onto people here and there, so as to find a hold.

I have learned and again pass it on: In the proximity of our spine there are seven spiritual centers of consciousness, which, like everything, have their order, so that they may also provide for our cell structure and the aura of the person.

Near our physical heart is the fourth consciousness center, also called the Christ-center. This center is my hold, to which I also direct my prayers. There, I also perceive the dialogue with nature or with the animals as energy, as a communication of consciousness.

Try it out. In time—and there is a time for everything—it will get easier for you. What do we say so succinctly? "It feels easier in my heart." If it is as it could be, you could then also say: "God touched me through the communication of consciousness with nature."

Thus, there is a time for everything!

In time, you become calmer and more self-assured. You want to be alone more often than before. It is possible that the world will suddenly find you odd and peculiar.

That is so, but you yourself are neither the one nor the other. You notice and feel a certain calmness and secureness in your thoughts and characteristic traits. Often you do not know yourself where that comes from.

A gentle remark from me: God is the stillness.

May I call your attention to the Lily? It symbolizes the purity, God's love, the security in God, the beauty through the love for the Being and not lastly, the freedom.

It grows, blooms and matures in the garden of God and, when it may, in your heart—indeed, for then, near your heart is the emerging Age of the Lily, the beginning of the New Era. Try, as often as possible, to go into the inner garden, for example, in prayer, in order to become still or to take your inner concerns to God, the eternal Father-Mother-God.

In this way, you will become ever calmer, whereby many thoughts will suddenly become unimportant. Your work goes more easily and your desire to take a walk every now and then—if possible, alone—brings fulfillment.

A walk will often encourage you to follow a certain path. If you feel like it, take it and watch what addresses you today and now, and what begins to communicate in the fourth center.

The question is: Who has sent to you; who wants to communicate with you?

This and much more is the beginning of the Age of the Lily. It is the preparation for the appearance of the light of the Christ of God, of the spiritual Messiah: "*I come soon.*"

If one considers what Christ, the Son of God, endured as Jesus of Nazareth, to release a part of His divine heritage and in the "It is finished," to protect the core of being in every soul with the heavenly power, then truly God-conscious people should also go toward Him, so that His work of bringing home all the sons and daughters of God may find completion.

Dear fellow people, the Age of the Lily has just begun. A brighter time will shine on the people of the next generations.

May the New Era, the Lily, Sophia, the Wisdom of God, already now blossom in all our hearts and may its purity and beauty encourage us to open our hearts to God in us.

In this awareness of the Lily—Sophia—at the beginning of the New Era,

Gabriele

We will be glad to send you
our current catalog of books, CDs and DVDs,
as well as free excerpts on many different topics

Gabriele Publishing House – The Word
P.O. Box 2221, Deering, NH 03244, USA
North America: Toll-Free No. 1-844-576-0937
International Orders: 49-9391-504-843
www.Gabriele-Publishing-House.com